GOOD GRIEF

PAMELA EVANS

Bird House Publishing

A Subsidiary of Bird House Enterprises LLC

8325 Broadway Street, Ste. 202 |Pearland, TX 77581 | (832) 535-2362

Bird House Publishing is committed to filling the need for more diverse books. We are also committed to the relentless pursuit of equity, authenticity, and inclusion. We encourage all of our readers and authors to show up in the world as their best selves. Our stories build empathy, coping skills, courage, and curiosity to explore cultures other than our own. We are always looking for diverse and thoughtful voices to share with the world.

ISBN: 978-1-7343217-7-7

Disclaimer: This book includes a collection of inspiration, encouraging words, and suggestions based on the author's personal experience. This book is not intended to represent professional psychology, psychiatry, counseling or therapy services. If you or someone you know is experiencing difficulty coping with loss or has had thoughts of self-harm or suicidal ideation please call the suicide prevention lifeline at 800-273-8255.

Bird House Publishing rev date 11/30/21

FOREWARD

The Covid-19 Pandemic was more than anyone could have expected when word of the virus first began trickling out. I had just begun work leading healthcare equity efforts in a major hospital system when the first surge descended on the Country. I have spent many years working in communities ravaged by poverty and lack of adequate grief counseling. Still, nothing prepared me for the sheer volume of almost universal grief that was ushered in as families were forced to separate completely from their sick, dead, and dying under the pandemic safety protocols. The basic human dignities and rites of passage to the next life that are the hallmarks of our civilization were restrained or refused for many families. Working closely with our chaplaincy teams and employee wellness we found ourselves in the trenches of grief from every side, serving as stand-ins for comfort that should have come from familial and community relationships. Personal loss also swiftly touched my own family and left me unmoored and devastated. In the midst of all of this, I was given the opportunity to serve as one of the early reviewers of this work by Pamela Evans. Reading these pages brought a sense of peace and comfort that can only come from the experience of knowing that someone really and truly understands what you are going through. In the words of Good Grief, I found my own experiences reflected and some of the questions I was still grappling with answered. It is truly a work of love, a light house standing in the storm, to guide you back to solid ground.

PROLOUGUE

My name is Pamela Evans. I am both fatherless and motherless. At 52 years old, I became an orphan. I wrote this book in the midst of one of the most painful times in my life. At a time when my heart was overwhelmed with grief, and I was in a dark place, full of pain and amid tragedy, I could not believe that God would give me a directive to write this book. I lost my mother less than one year after my father's death and about a week before I began writing this book. I know that a countless number of people have lost their mothers and fathers. That's a fact. But acknowledging that fact does not negate the pain I feel at this very moment.

Even as I wrote this book, many people reached out to me about their losses. Those contacts turned into a grief support group that I began hosting in-person and moderating online. As these exchanges increased, it became evident that the events, processes, and interactions that happen during grief are unique to every individual but walking through grief with others helped me grapple with my sorrow and established the sense of purpose from which this book was born.

It can be difficult to express the profound emotions that wash over you when coping with a loss. It can be even more difficult and complicated to try to express support for others that are grieving. So many times people do not reach out to support others that are grieving because they truly do not know what to say. It is my sincere hope that reading this book will allow you to become better equipped to handle both your grief as well as increase your ability to console those who are grieving. Use this book to help process your grief and return to it when you need inspiration, consoling, or help to find the right words to comfort a loved one.

Dedication

William D. Evans, my father

Clara M. Evans, my mother

Grace A. Robinson, my great aunt

Deborah Gorrell, my Philly mom

Poem: Complicated Grief

Sometimes grief hits you.

Sometimes grief grips you.

Rarely does it escape you.

Sometimes it covers you and saturates your soul.

Sometimes it submerges you, suffocates you and it extracts from you any hint of hope.

Grief drowns joy, it immobilizes the heart. It disguises itself as healing within the hippocampus of your mind.

Grief is life-altering; it's idiosyncratic; it is complicated.

Grief has been busy.

WHAT IS GRIEF?

In an effort toward common language, let's begin by defining some of the terms used in this book. This will ensure we are on the same page and understand from the same perspective.

Grief is described as a feeling of deep sorrow, especially one caused by someone's death. Grief is the constellation of internal thoughts and feelings we have when someone we love dies. In other words, grief is the internal meaning given to the experience of loss. It is an expression of love with no place to go. Mourning is when you take the grief you have on the inside and express it outside yourself.

What is good grief?

Good grief is sometimes referred to as normal or functional grief. It is healthy. It allows survivors to identify, acknowledge, and feel the loss they have suffered without self-isolation.

Good Grief!

Your friends and family may not be comfortable with grief and they will try to "make" you feel better. Know that you are allowed to tell them to let you grieve. It is healthy for you to do so. They may distance themselves, and that is okay. Don't judge them. They are doing what works for them and you must do what works for you. This does not make either of you a bad person.

What is mourning?

Mourning is said to be the expression of deep sorrow for someone who has died, typically following certain conventions such as wearing black clothes. It is the outward expression of grief. Depression, confusion, and the loss of interest in social activities are common when one is mourning.

The seven emotional stages of grief are usually understood to be the following:

1. Shock or disbelief
2. Denial
3. Bargaining
4. Guilt
5. Anger
6. Depression
7. Acceptance/hope

Symptoms of grief can be emotional, social, or religious in nature. Studies also show that grief can have a physical effect on the body. It can increase blood pressure and put one at risk for blood clots. It can alter the heart muscle, and it can cause what is known as broken heart syndrome. This is a disease that has the same symptoms as a heart attack. This is why it is very important for the griever to take care of themselves and for the consoler to be watchful of those who are experiencing grief.

Please note that these stages of grief were originally identified for the person who is in the midst of transition and is now deceased, not for who we know as the griever. Later, studies showed that the griever experiences similar emotions. The griever, however, may not experience them in that order and may actually skip a step or revisit a step more than once. It is a very individual process. It's an unwanted and unpredictable roller coaster ride for anyone who experiences it.

I encourage you to do your own research and explore the grief process more thoroughly. It will bless your life and if done right, it will bless others as well.

for the person who is in the midst of transition and is now deceased,
not for who we know as the present. Later, studies showed that the
griever experiences similar emotions. The grievers, however, may not
experience them in that order and may actually skip a step or revisit a
step more than once. It is a very individual process. It's an unwanted
and unpredictable roller coaster ride for anyone who experiences it.

I encourage you to do your own research and explore the grief
process more thoroughly. It will bless your life and if done right, it
will bless others as well.

From Caretaker to Taking Care

My mother, Clara Mae Evans, lived in Florence, SC. She is survived by two daughters, two grandchildren, and two great-grandchildren, and we all live in Philadelphia. My mother was one of the sweetest women that ever walked the earth. I don't say this because she was my mother. Many would attest to this fact. She was a quiet woman who loved everyone and would go out of her way to help those in need. She was an amazing cook. She didn't make a lot of fuss, but she moved a lot of mountains during her life. Clara was a faithful Christian woman. She served in her local church until her last day.

When we lost her in 2020, it was at the height of the first United States wave of the COVID-19 pandemic, and the world just was not making any sense. There was death everywhere. The media, both social and mainstream, was flooded with reports of death. It had gotten so bad that I stopped watching television in an attempt to escape the nonstop barrage of morbid news. Then, death visited my doorstep. My mom took ill and passed away. Now, my mother didn't die due to COVID, but it had such a major impact on us that it is important to mention it. While my mother was in the hospital, we were not allowed to visit her. All I could think of was her being in that hospital alone without her loved ones. The hospital was very busy due to the COVID pandemic. No one really had time to give extra care. The staff was limited and stressed. They were working 16-hour days just trying to complete their basic routines. While they were all gracious and caring to us, we realized that calling too many times a day would weigh heavily on them. They kindly allowed us to do video calls with my mom so she would know we were there. My sister and I would try to call only once or twice per shift to not overwhelm the nurses. It was one of the hardest things I had ever experienced.

My mother had battled both diabetes and kidney disease for years. Her health had declined to the point where she needed to get an amputation. Needless to say, she did not want to have that done. Her mother had experienced that, and my mother knew it would alter life as she knew it. She was a very independent woman. She worked until she was 70 years of age. Even after retirement, she worked tirelessly at her church and served in many capacities. She drove her dear aunt and best friend to all of the church district meetings and wherever their hearts desired to go. She knew that getting that amputation would change that. In fact, it is safe to say that she began to grieve the loss of her limb even before it was gone.

I remember about a month or so before her final visit to the hospital, she had gone in because her sugar level was too high. This was before the pandemic hit the country, so I was allowed to go with her. Each doctor that came in had news that seemed to get worse and worse. Knowing that her mother experienced the same surgery, some would say that she inherited this disease; personally, I believe she inherited poor self-care and eating habits which caused the disease to repeat itself.

At first, they said they had to take a few toes, then they said they would need to go as high as the middle of her foot, then to the ankle. Before you knew it, they were just above the knee. Each time a new report came in, I witnessed my mother's spirit drop deeper and deeper into a depression. I tried all I could to bring cheer but to no avail. She was in shock and denial and had initiated her own grieving over the inevitable loss of her limbs.

Grief doesn't just happen after a loss. It can very well start when you know the loss is near. My mother procrastinated for weeks upon weeks, moving from shock to denial. She tried different treatments and procedures with hopes that something would work. Well, nothing worked. According to medical professionals, if she didn't get the surgery, gangrene or sepsis would take over her body and she would die. At this point, she was in an enormous amount of pain and had become delusional. Despite my prayers, God had a different will for her life, and she ultimately had to get the amputation done in emergency surgery. It devastated her.

Her left leg was amputated just above the knee and three toes were amputated from the right foot. Mom, as we knew her, went downhill from there. My dear blessed mother, I believed, went into a deep state of depression, experiencing shock. We knew she didn't want to live life without her limbs. I believe that with all her other comorbidities, her body was not strong enough to undergo surgery. She suffered a stroke during surgery.

We felt that if, in fact, the doctors were right, and she was at the end of life, that we did not want her in a hospital alone without being surrounded by her family. Thankfully, at the suggestion of a cousin of mine, a nurse, we decided to bring my mother home on hospice care. Her independence had always been important to her. She never wanted to be a burden to anyone. She had stopped accepting food, denied a feeding tube, and was not responding well to directives. She began to accept that she was dying. I believe it was not only the stroke that killed her but also the heartbreak of having to lose her limb.

Though doubt still rises in my mind sometimes, I believe we made the right choice. My mother was surrounded by love, prayers, songs of praise. Present was our dear Aunt Grace, her best friend and mentor, her children, grandchildren, great-grandchildren, and family. She passed peacefully and without incident. I was and still am in shock. I truly did not believe that this was her time. I was sure God would deliver, but He didn't—at least not in the way I wanted anyway.

Have you ever rehearsed the testimony of victory? I mean really planned how you will tell the story of what the outcome would be. I did. No one could have convinced me that I would lose my mother just two weeks shy of the anniversary of my father's death. Though I knew amputation was a major operation, it is considered a standard one. The only complication I expected was her leg might heal slowly due to her diabetes. That's it. Never did I think that it would lead to her death. I felt a sense of guilt for convincing her to have the surgery.

Good Grief!

Note to self: Get your health in order. You don't want your children to experience watching you go through what you saw your mother go through.

Grief is unique in every instance; even if it's the same person grieving for multiple reasons.

I loved both of my parents dearly, but the experience was very different each time, and it was different when I mourned other loved ones. I remember when my grandmother passed away. I was seven months pregnant with my oldest child. I didn't properly grieve until about five years after her death. I was told "be strong" and "don't cry; you will put stress on the baby." In hindsight, I know this was not the right advice or choice.

12

Grievers must be compassionate too

Don't judge those who are absent. Love and appreciate the ones that are there. Grief is hard for everyone—those personally affected and those who care about the mourners. When I lost my mother, there were those who called and others encouraged, and I am grateful to have people who cared enough to reach out. Some people called that I least expected and some I thought would call didn't. Mourners, you must be okay with this fact. It will happen. Just a year before, I lost my father to a vicious disease called Huntington's. Again, I say it was a very different experience. There were those I thought would be there by my side but were not, and then there were those who I never thought would be there that were. What I learned from these experiences is that you cannot take people's responses personally. There are several reasons why this happens.

The first reason, and probably the most common, is that most people do not know how to respond to grief. It is not taught in school unless one goes to school specifically for grief counseling. Unfortunately, it is not taught in the church. Again, unless you have trained grief counselors, it is usually not a well-thought-out strategic plan on how to handle those experiencing grief.

The second reason is an unintentional lack of compassion. This happens when one has not experienced a deep grief caused by the loss of a loved one, so, quite simply, they are unable to identify with your grief. A sister in my church lost her father. She was someone who was loved greatly and had a lot of love and support around her during her time of bereavement. She had a strong village. After the funeral was over and the fanfare had ceased, I watched her as she fought to go back to her normal routine. It was expected that she would just pick

13

up where she left off. I could see, through the spirit of discernment, that she was not ready to go back to business as usual. I didn't say anything to her, but I prayed silently that someone in her inner circle would recognize this and that she would have the strength to speak out to say, "Wait! I am not okay," or "I'm not ready."

The third and final reason you should not take it personally when you feel people do not show up for you in your period of grief is that they may be overwhelmed. We will never truly know what people have going on in their lives. We do not know the battles one faces on a daily basis, and just because someone does not come to your griever's table does not mean they do not care. It doesn't even mean they don't understand, and it's certainly not proof that they don't mean well. Consider this: their life load may already be too much to bear. If they accept even a spoonful of your grief, they just may bust open. In some cases, it is best for them to stay away.

When I lost my mother, the entire country was engulfed in not only the 2020 COVID-19 pandemic but also the growing outrage at systemic injustices plaguing black and brown communities. Protests and riots raged on both in the U.S. and abroad. There was mistrust growing for not only law enforcement but medical personnel as the disparity in pandemic death rates became directly correlated to ethnicity. Massive layoffs began and businesses closed their doors, unable to survive stay-home safety orders. There was a sense of collective fear, mistrust, stress, and confusion.

Though these things may not be going on where you are when you read this book, it is very possible that some of the people in your life may be suffering from their own personal trauma or experiencing private crises or chaos. Perhaps they do not have the emotional bandwidth to deal with your grief at this moment. Perhaps they, too, are grieving. It may be at the loss of a loved one, a job, a home, or a spouse. It could be so many things. Don't be too quick to judge or cut off a person that is not there for you in your grief. Simply love and appreciate the ones who are.

Selfish Love

Is it selfish of us to not want to experience the death of a loved one? I would have rather died before my parents so as not to have experienced the pain of losing them, despite knowing that they would have to experience the pain of losing a child. Is it okay for us to want them to experience the pain so we don't have to? For me, this was a very sobering thought.

While the dying has no control over their appointed time, they have a way of protecting their survivors. When my dad died, my sister and I were sitting with him by his side for hours. We got hungry, so my sister stepped out to make a quick run to grab us a bite to eat. Fifteen minutes after she walked out, he took his last breath. Coincidentally or not, a similar scenario happened with my mother. My sister had been there all day long, and the moment she left to pick up some medicine for my mom, about 15-20 minutes later, my mother passed. Were they protecting her?

I still hear the sound of my father's final breath at night. I am not sure if I was in the room when my mom took her last breath. I believe I knew it, but I did not want to record it in my mind. Either I walked in just after it happened, or I was there and refused to accept it. I remember walking in and out of the room. Sitting down and getting back up. I was a nervous wreck. My aunt looked at me, trying her best not to say she was gone, and I walked out of the room as if leaving would change the outcome. It didn't become real to me until my aunt mustered up enough strength to get up and close my mother's mouth because she was very adamant about making sure her mouth or eyes did not freeze open. It was at that moment that shock hit me like a lightning bolt. I did one of the most stupid things one could do. I knew better, but shock made me do it. I called my sister and asked if she had reached the drug store yet. She had just pulled into the parking lot. Knowing she was alone and behind the wheel, I told her. "Well don't waste your money. She doesn't need it." For just that moment I was concerned about her losing $60-70 dollars more than I was for the safety of my sister. I still regret that moment to this day. She had to ride back to the house knowing her mother had just passed, and she had no one with her to lean on. This has got to be the biggest regret I carry. "Why would I do something so ridiculous?" I said to myself. I should have waited until she got back home and told her when she had support around her. I did the same stupid thing when my dad passed. I hope that my sister can forgive me.

Be careful how you break the news to loved ones. Make sure they have a support system around them. It is not good for them to be alone, and it is worse to tell them over the phone. I know sometimes it can't be avoided, but in my case, it could have, and I was not a responsible bearer of bad news either time. My pastor has often said, "some say that experience is the best teacher; but I say someone else's experience is the best teacher." Please learn from my experience. Be deliberate in your delivery when it comes to relaying a message of someone's death. All I could think was, "what if my sister gets into an accident on her way back to the house?" I would have never been able to forgive myself. I am grateful to God she didn't, but I have asked God to never let me make that type of mistake again. While it was not my intent to be insensitive, it was a completely insensitive act.

16

Years ago, when my friend's mom passed away, I was given the task to go through her telephone book and call her friends to tell them of her passing. What a task it was! Some people literally burst into tears and sulked when I told them. Others just hung up the phone on me, and others asked the old reflex response question: "Are you serious?" By the time I got to the end of that phone book, I was totally exhausted. I had become a counselor, a sounding board, a therapist, a burden bearer, etc. I had to become so many of the things I didn't want to be in that moment, but when you offer help, see it through. It is not always comfortable or convenient. I wanted to pass that job over after the first uncontrollable outburst, but I labored through it because I said I would. That's called integrity. That's called friendship. That's called ministry.

Folks, Family, and Frustrations

Let's address the elephant in the room. When folks die, things can get bad! People start fighting about who is in charge, who is going to get what, who was there for their loved one and who was not; who is paying for what, and who is at fault. I am extremely grateful that I only have one sibling and we are both civilized and agreeable people. This was a blessing. When my dad died. It was as if there was an unspoken agreement that I'd take the lead, and when my mom died, she would. That is exactly what happened. Together, we were able to block out a lot of the nonsense that tried to enter our atmosphere because we stood together in unity and transparency—no secrets and no hidden agendas. We all know that is not how it always plays out.

Folks will try you. They become very blind to the fact that you are grieving. Greed is blinding. They ask for items that belong to the deceased. They ask about wills and the amount of money you will get. I, especially, was in awe of people when my mother passed.

Folks wanted pots, clothes, hats, pills, and ointments. You name it! I understand that people may want some type of memento to remember the deceased, but one day after their passing is not the time to make that request. Don't be insensitive. Now, if the bereaved mentions it or offers it, great. Go with it. But for you to part your lips to ask at such a time tells the griever that "things" are more important than the life and loss of your loved one. You don't want to send that message. Be wise in your asking. If you offer proper consolation, the griever might want you to have something of their loved ones simply because you cared enough to minister to them at such a difficult time.

I belong to a family that owns land in the south. Our family is very proud and protective of that land and rightfully so. Our great-grandparents sowed a lot of sweat and tears to obtain that land. It is well known within the family that we must never sell the land to anyone who is not a blood relative. I have witnessed all-out blowouts among other families after someone's death. Families fought about whose land belongs to who, how one family member traded land with another, and how this one wanted to steal the other's land. This has happened at impromptu meetings on the day of the funeral of the deceased! One time, my family actually held two separate repasts after a funeral because they just could not put aside their differences.

Some of you may say, "why is she exposing her family business?" Some of my family may be annoyed that I mentioned this, but no one can deny the reality of it. What I do know is that my family is not the only family that has experienced this. Usually, when this happens, it stems from something deeply rooted from years back. The folks arguing don't even have the full truth of why the rivalry exists. There is usually some truth to everyone's argument, and it will continue until someone is bold enough to face it head-on and in love, or humble

18

enough to let it go in wisdom. If neither of those things happens, it will continue to live in our families.

Sibling rivalry goes back to nearly the beginning of time. Look at the story of Cain and Abel or Esau and Jacob. God does not wish that siblings fight with one another. He wants us to live in harmony and love one another, especially during hard times such as death.

> "Behold, how good and pleasant it is when brothers dwell in unity."
>
> Psalms 133:1
>
> "Finally, all of you, have unity of mind, sympathy, brotherly love, a tender heart, and a humble mind."
>
> 1 Peter 3:8

In the above passage of scripture, God is not only talking about your brothers and sisters in Christ, your sorority sisters, or your lodge brothers. He is also talking about your biological siblings and your family. We do realize that the Word of God is for the just as well as the unjust. Even if you or your family do not identify as believers, the Word still stands as a message for peace for us all. God's desire for us to follow peace with all (wo)men does not change based on the maturity of our faith or the length of our level of spirituality. Christ is quite clear about how a family should treat one another. Family is one of the first institutions God established for human interaction. He tells husbands to love their wives and wives to submit to their husbands. He charges children to obey their parents and parents not to provoke their children to wrath.

> "But if anyone does not provide for his relatives, and especially for members of his household, he has denied the faith and is worse than an unbeliever."
>
> 1 Timothy 5:8

God actually cares about how we treat our family. When the rivalry within your family starts to rear its ugly head, remember that if you say you are a Christian then you should endeavor to be Christ-like. Jesus endured much for the sake of unity. In 1 Peter 2:23, it says "[the Jewish religious leader and Roman guards] hurled their insults at him, and he did not retaliate, when he suffered, he made no threats." Know that when we don't do right by our family, God is not pleased.

Funeral Wishes and Preparations

There are a few things I would like to share about this. First, to the consoler, do not push your desires and ideas onto the griever. Giving your unsolicited advice or suggestions about how things should be done is not your place. Understand that this is already a difficult process. Refrain from giving your opinion unless it is requested. I'm talking about things like the outfit the deceased will wear, which professional services to use, and what the color theme should be. Those things should be handled by the person designated to handle those particulars. It is a very sensitive topic, and your opinion should not be at the forefront. Perhaps leaving them with a pamphlet or a checklist might be helpful, but this is not the time for you to vicariously plan your own or your loved one's funeral.

To the griever, I say be as sober-minded as possible. We know you loved the deceased but be wise. Take along someone you trust when handling business so as not to be taken advantage of. Unfortunately, handling the deceased is a big business, and, just like any other salesperson, the funeral home staff will try and sell you the expensive products and services. Try to do some research before you go to make final arrangements. Make a list. Shop around. Just because you consult with one funeral home does not obligate you to use them. Some of us have a particular funeral home that our family uses all the time, and that is good, but make sure it works for you. This is not the time to be a people-pleaser.

To the family, I say that unless you are contributing funds during this process, the decisions are not up to you. Be someone who handles your grieving loved ones with respect and care; not someone who wants to rush them because they are numb to the process.

When planning the funeral, here are some questions to think about when planning how to honor the deceased.

- Who else should be considered in this process?

  o Is there a dear friend or relative you should include?

  o Is there an ex-spouse that should be considered?

  o Are there any distant children or relatives that need to be notified?

  o Will it be a funeral, a homegoing, a memorial, or some other name?

  o Will they have a burial, which means they are placed in a casket and then placed in the ground? Or will they be entombed, which means they are placed in a casket and then placed in a mausoleum or crypt?

- ○ Will they be cremated? If so, will their ashes be spread abroad, or will they be put in an urn? Who will keep the urn? Will it stay in someone's home, or will it be placed in the cemetery?

  - ○ What rituals or practices does their faith dictate? Were they Jewish? Muslim? Christian?

- What is your budget?

- What venue is suitable for the occasion?

- Did the deceased have any final wishes?

- Have you released all your personal bias as it relates to notices, invitations, and participation to reflect the wishes of the deceased?

- Will you purchase needed items from the funeral home, or can you buy wholesale?

- Will they wear something out of their own closet, or do you want to purchase something new?

- Will you purchase clothing from the funeral home?

- Who will do the deceased's hair and makeup? Will it be the funeral home or maybe the deceased normal hairstylist/makeup artist?

- How many guests might be in attendance?

- How many programs will be needed? Do you even want to have a program?

As you see, the decisions can be overwhelming, and this list is not exhaustive. There are so many intricate details to planning a memorial or homegoing service, and it is wise to have a trusted companion there to help you sort out all the options.

The most well-organized funeral planning process that I have ever witnessed was the mother of a friend. I was actually living in her home at the time of her mother's death. Her mom had planned her entire funeral from beginning to end. She selected her outfit, chose where her professional services would be rendered, picked out the casket, took the photo she wanted to use to the funeral home, pre-paid for her service, and wrote out the obituary. All we had to do was insert the date of death and hit print. I learned so much from that experience. It took so much pressure off the family. This freed them up to grieve and not be consumed with the details of planning a funeral.

I used to think that people did not want to talk about their death wishes because they thought they were going to live forever. Being in the midst of this pandemic, where loss is happening at an alarming rate, my thoughts have been slightly altered. I think the thought of death is just too painful, even to those of us who profess to have hope in Christ. Most families don't want to have this conversation, but it is so important. If you have a loved one for whom you might be responsible for planning their homegoing, try to have them write down their wishes. It can be a difficult or uncomfortable situation but a very necessary one. I encourage you to take the time to write down your desires as well. This allows your loved ones to experience "good grief" and not to be consumed with the tedious task of figuring out the details.

When planning my mother's funeral, we were faced with an unprecedented situation. Because of the pandemic, we were only allowed to have seven people attend the funeral. That included the minister who was officiating the service. This was devastating! She had two children, two grandchildren, and two great-grandchildren. She also had six living siblings. How were we to choose which siblings would attend? We ended up having to leave the younger grandchild and the great-grandchildren home and the sibling part worked out only because some of them lived in New York which was shut down at the time, and they were not permitted to leave the city to travel to my mother's funeral. But things could have become tense if we'd had to make more cuts to who could attend. These are decisions one should not have to make when mourning the loss of a loved one. For those of you that did have to grapple with these decisions and make hard choices, please forgive yourself. You did your best. Do not hold onto a regret that is not yours to carry.

Good Grief!

Note: Pre-planning is a selfless act. It is one of the best things you can do for your loved ones. Except the Lord come, we all must cross that path. It is inevitable.

Say Thank You

This is an important part of the process. Saying "thank you" lets the consoler know that their presence mattered. It lets them know that they did something right. A "thank you" in the moment is good, but a "thank you" during the aftermath is more effective.

Consider that you have lost a loved one, and one of your friends was there to support you 100% of the way through. They were there from the time you got the call until the moment your loved one was put to rest. They cooked, cleaned, and contributed. I'm sure you gave a verbal "thank you" when they brought the meal to you or when they

24

picked up the obituaries so you would not have to go out. You know that it is all done from the heart. Friends like that really don't need a thank you. It's simply understood, right? Wrong! Friends or consolers like this should especially be thanked. They probably have sacrificed a lot of time and resources, and maybe even neglected their own family to be there for you. They should get a different type of card; not the ones from the funeral home that they probably helped you fill out.

During the pandemic, I became better acquainted with technology. When I reminisced about all who were there to help me, I wanted to find a way to let them know how much I appreciated their presence during such a difficult time. At a time when I could not hug or converse face-to-face with anyone, I sent personalized e-cards to say, "thank you." Also remember that it is never too late to say, "thank you," no matter how long it takes. It matters.

Poem: Guilt & The Blame Game

The most hurtful yet common game in the face of grief.

I blame you, You blame me, We blame them, They blame us, We all blame God.

Who wins the game?

In the midst of the pandemic-

I experience a personal crisis.

Corona has come into our land, and she is abusive, she's a thief and a terrorist

In the midst of a pandemic- I grieve, I hurt. Are you alone? I am alone.

I'm blinded by truth and reality

I hear only the crashing sound of my faith-filled prayers hitting a brick wall.

I feel numb, joy or contentment are no more

My belly cannot stomach acceptance. It's unpalatable.

It is undesirable, unimaginable, and unattainable.

In an attempt to soothe my aching heart; I medicate myself with dose after dose of empty ventures, hollow relationships, and a bit of retail therapy.

The relationships have dissolved, and the money is gone.

Yet the pain never stops, we must learn to just manage it.

LIVING WITH GRIEF

The Father's Day shortly after my own father's passing was the worst day. My whole being was shaken. We all know that Father's Day gets nowhere near the attention that Mother's Day gets. There are no overwhelming amounts of commercials or store sales. No one is on the corner selling Father's Day boutonnieres. It's just a day, and, unless you personally make it special, it kind of comes and goes without much fuss. Well, this particular year, I don't know if the media upped the ads or if the fuss was in my mind. The torment I experienced was agonizing. It seemed that everywhere I turned, there was a reminder that Father's Day was approaching. I dreaded the coming of this day, and I contemplated what I would do on this day. Would I stay in bed all day and cry? Would I smash my car into a brick wall? Would I pop some pills and sleep the day away? My emotions were all over the place, and that was scary

I don't recall anyone saying to me or acknowledging that this would be a hard day for me to handle. Somehow, I found enough strength to get out of bed and make it to church. I'm still not sure how. I truly don't even remember how I got dressed or how I got to church. I guess by being a creature of habit, my body was on autopilot. I sat outside in the car and contemplated going back home. Finally, I pulled myself together, wiped my face, and I walked in like a wet sponge. I refused to look anyone in the face.

I prayed that no one would ask the casual question of "how are you doing?" I knew that if I had any personal interactions that I'd completely fall apart. As I walked to my seat, tears rolled down my face. I cried throughout the entire praise and worship session. I wasn't crying as an act of worship. I was hurting. I missed my daddy. Then, in the midst of the praise session, I was interrupted by a deacon who, coincidentally, had recently lost his father. He asked me to lead the prayer.

Everything in me said no. My heart said no; my mind said no; my soul said no. Everything but my mouth. *What? Sir, don't you know it's Father's Day, and I just lost my father, I'm not praying. Get a man to pray. I'm not even sure I'm talking to God for myself, let alone on behalf of these people. No, sir!* My mind prepared that entire response, but my mouth did not say one word of it. Instead, I said, "okay." I was so mad at my mouth that day. Have you ever had your mouth turn on you? I turned cold at the thought of going up to that podium, knowing I was a whole wreck. Again, being a creature of habit and being obedient, I went up to pray. I was sure someone would have to come and take over because I would fall apart at the seams before I got a word out. But God!

God gave me a supernatural strength to pray, and, at that moment, I realized that it wasn't about me. It was about all the others in that church that were going through the same emotions as I was. I wasn't the only one who had lost their father that year. Mine may have been a little more recent than others, but it did not negate the fact that there were more "virgins" in the building. Other people were experiencing their first Father's Day without their father.

What I realized is that it wasn't enough to simply say, in passing, that we pray for those who no longer have their fathers during a message or during a moment of exhortation. We needed someone to earnestly pray for us. We needed to know that someone understood our pain. We needed to know that it was okay to not be okay.

Good Grief!

Note to self: Try to be more intentional with your consolation efforts. It isn't just needed in the first week of a loss. It's needed continually, especially on those Virgin Days. Get an obituary, if you can, and note the death date and date of birth. Put it in your phone to remind you to be there for that person as they approach those milestones.

Facing Your "Virgin Days"

How do you face the very first anniversary of your loved one's death? How much of the sadness will bubble back to the surface?

You will have what I call "Virgin Days." These are your loved one's first heavenly birthday, your first holiday without them, and the anniversary of their death. Virgin Days are the moments that silently torment us as they approach. Most people don't recognize that your loved one's birthday is nearing or that the anniversary of their death has come. These are the times when storm-like emotions rise up within your heart and mind. A day that only you really know about. The average consoler has moved past your loss. Even a good and proper one rarely remembers the important milestones you will encounter for the next year ahead.

My father died a few weeks before his birthday and two weeks later was Father's Day. The same happened with my mother. She died about a week before her birthday and Mother's Day was a few days later. This can be a good and a bad thing. Good because there were still people there to surround us with support as it was still fresh in their minds. In my mother's case, we had not laid her to rest yet, so the consolers were still present. Her birthday became a part of the "culminating activities" if you will. For me, with both my mom and my dad, the most significant Virgin Days came immediately following their death.

When you approach these milestones after the passing of a loved one, you usually walk that road alone unless you have someone who is divinely connected to you. The interesting thing I found was that it happens innately. One day you wake up, and you are sad. You don't even know why, and, suddenly, something reminds you that today is that day. It could be their date of departure, their birthday, anything. Something in your heart tells you to grieve again.

Consolers forget that first Easter or Thanksgiving dinner. They don't realize why you have lost your zeal for Christmas or any celebratory activities. It is because our lives are not the same. There is an empty place in our hearts. There is a missing component to that celebration, and it hurts like hell. My birthday, their birthday, special trips, and special places that we shared are not the same. Going to those places and participating in those activities are now painful.

When my dad first passed, I could not go on Lincoln Drive. That's the route I took when I went to visit him in his nursing home. When I got the call to come because his condition had worsened, I took that drive, and it was the longest, most excruciating ride ever. To this day, it hurts every time I find myself on the drive. No one knew this before now, and I have only once mentioned it. I just quietly avoid it so as to not feel the pain. There are things like this that grievers go through. I know I am not the only one because, since then, I have heard others say how they hate going to a particular hospital because their loved one died there. I have heard them say, "I don't drive down that street because my loved one was killed there." Those Virgin Days are very real.

For those who experienced loss during the pandemic, you may feel that you were not able to commemorate their lives in a manner worthy of their place in your heart, even as those important days continued to pass you by due to social distancing and other restrictions. Again, accept what was out of your control, and remain confident that you will have other opportunities to honor those losses.

Good Grief!

Having weird dreams? It is normal. When my dad passed, I had all kinds of weird dreams. I really didn't share it with anyone. I literally thought I was going crazy. I was shocked to hear my sister mention she had experienced the same thing when our mom passed. Most of my dreams did not make sense to me. In my limited research on death and dreams, the one common factor I found is that it is a part of the healing process. Dreams can comfort, soothe, and heal the mourner. Again, it is normal! Don't keep it to yourself. Find a confidant and share it. I encourage you to dream on and be healed.

I still have many Virgin Days to conquer. My mother passed at a time when I still had not completed my Virgin Days for my dad. No one knows your inner struggles during those times. My family decided to honor my dad on his first birthday after he passed, and we celebrated by going to his favorite restaurant and ordering his favorite items. This celebration was demanded by my spunky little granddaughter who was six at the time. I don't think any of us wanted to do this, but we understood that this was her way of honoring her Pop-Pop, so we all went along with the program as she desired. After dinner, we released balloons, and we sang "Happy Heavenly Birthday" to my dad. It was painful and no one knew the tears that I shed behind closed doors that evening. I survived. We survived.

Sober Drunk

One thing I have found to be common in the aftermath of grief is that one tends to try to medicate their sorrow with some form of soothing activity which is usually unhealthy. This ranges from anything from over shopping to hibernation/isolation, or even excessive exercising. One of the most common that I have found— and have actually succumbed to—is looking for companionship to fill the void of a lost loved one. Everyone wants to be loved. Now there is a hole in your heart.

Though you may be drunk with grief, refrain from making life-altering decisions while in your drunkenness. Avoid making large purchases such as houses or cars. Be sober when making decisions, especially as it pertains to relationships. Be careful to guard your heart. Men: don't lean in the wrong direction. A mere woman cannot bear the burden of a grieving heart. Women: a mere man cannot fill the void of your loved one. So many wrong relational decisions have come out of moments of grief. Then one day you sober up and find yourself in an entanglement, which is not healthy for your well-being.

I recommend that you engage yourself in an alternate activity such as taking a cooking class or painting course, both of which can be therapeutic. Take those music lessons you always wanted to indulge in. These types of activities are not harmful and are not permanent. If at any time they become overwhelming, you can just let them go. The same is not true for relationships or major purchases.

Poem: Will they Pray

As I scroll down my social media platforms, I see

post after post filled with fear, desperation, and tragedy.

I see sentiments of broken hearts, the bonds of hope and faith falling apart.

I feel the heaviness of the hearts of those who are soliciting prayers, venting frustration, and sounding alarms saying I am not okay!

Under those posts, I see empty words...empty as a glass of cold water on a hot summer day.

I see praying hands and crying emojis that indicate that we empathize and sympathize and for them, we will pray.

In a moment I experienced a jolt of raw revelation and from this jolt ignited a dose of pure and secret transparency. A still small voice enters my soul with two heart-wrenching questions...Have you prayed? Will you pray? My soul knoweth well that the effectual fervent prayers of the righteous availeth much; yet the continuous state of depression and oppression flooding my timeline hath not confirmed a prevailing power. We must build a prayer tower.

Since when did the pledge to...become as effective as a vow kept?
Selah

Will you really pray?

THE CALL TO CONSOLE

What is a consoler?

A consoler is a person who comforts another during a time of grief or mourning.

To be an effective consoler, it would do you and the griever well to have some knowledge of what the griever is experiencing. The purpose of a consoler is to ease the distress, not to magnify or add to it. You do not have to have experienced grief to be effective, but it does help to understand your role. I also have some rules for consolers to show up for their loved ones in a compassionate way.

Good Grief!

Knowledge is power. You never know when you will need it. The more you learn about the phases and symptoms of loss and grief, the more natural it becomes to support others walking through their own grief.

Rule 1: Let the griever NOT be okay

Please stop telling someone in mourning to hold on, not cry, and to be strong. It is not healthy advice. The Bible clearly tells us that there is a time to mourn. Read Ecclesiastes chapter 3 if you don't believe me.

35

> "…a time to weep and a time to laugh, a time to mourn and a time to dance…"
>
> Ecclesiastes 3:4 NIV

Now don't get me wrong; they need encouragement. They also need to know that there are better days ahead.

What a person experiencing grief also doesn't need to hear is your own personal grief story; especially if it was a non-comparable experience or one that was not very recent.

Let me explain briefly. If someone's mother passed away and is grieving, you should not tell them about your dear aunt who passed away 17 years ago, especially if your mother is still living. You may have really loved your aunt, and it may have hurt your heart, but the two incidents are not comparable. Even if your aunt raised you, the pain is far removed, and the current griever does not care. They won't tell you this, but I will tell you: we do not care about the death of your aunt 17 years ago.

Good Grief!

Note: Your pain does not ease my pain!

That being said, there are times when sharing a grieving experience is helpful. When my mother passed, one of my church sisters had just lost her mother about a week or two before. I had called to comfort her, and she expressed her appreciation. When my mother passed a week or so later, she called me. She shared that she understood the pain I felt and that it was an indescribable feeling. She said she didn't know how she was going to move past that moment, and I could relate. This, my friend, was helpful to know. My blinding grief was not solo to my

36

experience. I was not weak just because I didn't know how to navigate through my grief. I was simply blinded by the pain.

Please know that it is not easy to move on when you lose someone who has been part of your life forever, intricately woven into your daily schedule. Grievers will not tell you this, but I am screaming from the roof top for them: STOP! We are not ready to move on yet! We hurt. We want to hear their voice. We want to hug them. Grief is a very painful experience. When you undergo a heart operation, you don't just get up the next day and live life as you did the days before. Healing needs to take place. You have to be careful how much you lift; how much you move about. You can't do any strenuous activity until the doctor clears you to do so. It is the same in the spirit. When a piece of your heart is removed, it takes time to pick up the load of life again. I was so surprised to find out that my employer only gave four days for the bereavement of a parent. It is an injustice to both the griever and the employer. If you are in a field of service, it is an injustice to those you serve. You are not going to get a well-tuned employee after just four days. In most cases, it's not even enough time to bury your loved one. The healing process must take its course. Please give the griever time to recover, and the recovery doesn't begin until the fanfare ends.

Rule 2: Be mindful of what you say

People say the darkest things. Many don't know what to say and what not to say to a griever. When someone is grieving, you should refrain from saying the following:

1. **Don't Cry. Be Strong**. Crying is inward grief pouring out and becoming mourning. It is healthy and should be encouraged. They don't need to be strong. You lend your strength. Let them lean on you for this moment.

37

2. **They're in a better place or God loved them best.** Though biblically, it may be true, all a griever knows is that the better place to be is here, on earth, with them. We all feel that we have enough love to conquer anything the now deceased may have been going through. This reality should be left to the griever to decide. Please refrain from using this statement. It does not help. This bears repeating: IT DOES NOT HELP!

3. **At least you don't have to take care of them anymore or I'm sure it's a burden lifted off of you.** If you have ever said these words to anyone, praise your God if you didn't get slapped or cussed all the way out. This is one of the most insensitive things a "consoler" can say.

4. **Did they leave you any money?** In true and pure grief, material things become obsolete. Please don't ask about inheritances or money unless you intend on significantly contributing to the cause. Even then, just ask them to pass you a bill so you can take care of it. It is not your business if the deceased left anything behind.

5. **What are you going to do with their belongings?** Folks were asking these questions before my mom's body was cold. Again, if you have asked this question, thank your lucky stars you have all your teeth in your mouth! It's rude and insensitive.

6. **Did they have a will?** My counter-reaction to this is, "Am I in your will?" Go have several seats with your nosey self. The only people that have a right to know this are those who are handling the affairs. If that is not you, mind your business!

7. **How much money did they have in their account?** Once again, I'll answer this with a counter-question: How much are

you offering to the account? Nothing? Okay, madame. Okay, sir. Mind your business.

8. **God never gives us more than we can handle**. I'm going to just say this on behalf of all the grievers: in the midst of grief, that is exactly what life feels like – more than we can handle. While it is biblically true, this truth is not particularly comforting amid grief.

9. **At least they lived a long life.** While I can understand the intention behind this sentiment, it draws unnecessary comparisons that highlight how sad we are or are not allowed to be based on the age of the deceased. This feels very much like we do not have permission to mourn fully. Ultimately, it does not often comfort the griever. You just don't ever feel that you had enough time with someone you love.

10. **How are you doing?** While this is one of the most sensible questions, can you really handle the answer? Most of us can't. Let's see... I am heartbroken. I'm full of sorrow. I'm in agony. I'm numb. I'm tired of your stupid questions. I'm exhausted. Should I go on? How do you think I am doing? There is a hole in my heart! Only ask this question if you have time and opportunity to settle in and really listen to any and everything that spills out.

11. **Are you serious?** I learned this early in life. It's a natural but jarring reaction to hearing the news of someone's death, especially when it was sudden. Ever get that call? "Hi, it's me. Just calling to let you know that [a loved one] passed away." The person on the other end of the phone says, with great sincerity, "Are you serious!?" No, it's a game I'm playing

today! It happens, and I've been guilty. So have many of you, too. It's a horrible first reaction because who would joke in that manner? That is so inappropriate. Our mouths often betray us when we are shocked by hard news. Try to avoid this knee-jerk reaction.

12. **I know how you feel**. Rarely do we really know how someone feels, even if we have experienced a deep loss of the same nature. All relationships are different, and everyone experiences their own phases and stages. Levels of grief are driven by relational filters. You don't really know how one feels. Even if they tell you, their expression of grief is more likely limited in comparison to what they truly feel. Only a master communicator can effectively and accurately convey their most inward emotions. Being emotionally overwhelmed affects one's ability to accurately disseminate their feelings. Don't say you know because, most likely, you *don't*.

13. **Call me if you need me**. Let me first say that I am, again, guilty of saying this. You do know they won't call. In most cases, they don't even know what they need. You have to use some foresight and determine what they may need. If they didn't express a need the first time you spoke with them, call again the next day or the next day. Offer specific services. Ask non- badgering questions. *Have you eaten? Do you need food? Do you have water? Are the kids okay? Can I take them to the park for a while? Do you need a ride somewhere to take care of some business?* These things are helpful and tell the person that your words are not idle. This lets them know that you really want to be present in the process.

Some of these may seem a bit outlandish, but these are just a few statements that were said to me at the passing of my parents. Please take a moment to think before you approach a griever. It is okay to rehearse what you will say even if you have to write down your words prior to talking to them. Remember, the goal is to comfort them, not to further damage their heart or to agitate their emotional state. You do more damage saying stupid stuff than not saying anything at all. Therefore, if you think you have the propensity to say something stupid, just send a card.

People want to know that you can be present with them in their pain. Saying and doing nothing says a lot too. If you don't have the words, then allow your actions to speak for you. Clean the house, send a meal, offer to run an errand for them. Do something constructive and helpful. Anything but a stupid thing is the best thing. It's likely not stupidity, but ignorance. Just the same, be intentional with your consolation efforts.

On the other hand, these are things that are both practical and helpful that you can say:

1. I can't imagine how you must feel.

2. There are no words.

3. How you are feeling is normal.

4. You are not going crazy.

5. Cry if you need to.

6. I wish there was something I could do to ease your pain.

7. This may hurt for a long time. Know that I am here to listen to you today, tomorrow and for years to come. Grief has no expiration date.

41

8. I'm really sorry you have to go through this.

9. It's okay to have bad days. It's expected when you lose someone you love.

10. Feel free to talk about your loved one as much or as little as you want to. I'm here.

11. Are there any errands I can take off your hands?

12. Have you eaten? What do you need at the house? Do you have enough water or beverages?

13. You can feel really good about how you took such great care of your loved one. They knew how much you loved them.

Rule 3: Think practically

Think about normal daily duties and see how you can relieve the griever of simple tasks.

I remember my cousin did something so impactful after the passing of my mother. I have an 11-year-old son who is a mama's boy (I reluctantly admit this). He is also a lover of basketball. Due to this COVID-19 pandemic, all recreational activities were shut down. We were in a small town in the south where there wasn't much to do in the first place. Here he is, a city kid, stuck deep in the country, with a mother who, due to her overwhelming grief, had become temporarily disengaged. Well, my cousin did the best thing ever. She has three grandsons who also love basketball. They had two portable courts at home. She had someone bring one of the courts to the home where we were staying so my son would have something to keep him occupied. She also brought the boys to keep him company. This very simple gesture was such a load lifted from me. I could focus on being an active participant in the planning of my mother's homegoing services because I didn't have to be concerned about what my son was doing. I knew he would be on that court morning, noon, and night. I would dare to say that it was also therapeutic for him in the midst of all that was taking place. Helping kids deal with grief is another topic for another book. Please note, however, kids grieve too. It should be appropriately addressed.

Another thing to be conscious of is overtaxing the griever. Be conscious of the amount of time you spend in their presence and help to protect their private time. Don't show up early in the morning unless they request it. More likely, they didn't get a good night's rest. Don't stay too late in the evening, again, unless they request it. Grieving is exhausting both mentally and physically.

I had two other cousins, a married couple, who helped. They showed up every day, not too early, and didn't stay too late. They made sure my family and I ate every single day. They bought the food, cooked it, and cleaned up every day. I was so grateful for them. I always loved them, but I tell you my love for them deepened after seeing how they stayed by our side, day in and day out. They made sure the kids were good. They printed out homework sheets for my son's virtual learning assignments. They provided kid-friendly meals like pizza and tacos. They were absolutely amazing! This taught me a lot about how to be present for a griever. They were not overbearing at all. I am grateful for the lessons learned through their service to me and my family.

Lastly, there was my dear Uncle David. He came by each morning to see what we needed, and then he came back each night to take out the trash and make sure we were okay. There were so many others whose presence made such a difference. I want to point this out: most of those deeds didn't cost anything. Don't allow the fact that you don't have extra money to stop you from being an amazing consoler. Consolation doesn't always require cash. The value is in the pure time and the sincerity of effort given.

In so many instances, people asked me if I needed anything, and the truth is that I didn't know what I needed until it was presented to me. At that moment, all I needed was for my loved one not to be gone. That's it! As a griever, my mind was all over the place. I didn't know if I was coming or going; sane or insane; normal or abnormal. I was in a cloud trying to function in the reality of life on earth. The interesting thing about those acts of kindness was that I didn't even know to ask for that type of help.

When my father passed, there were not a lot of visitors. In fact, the visitors were quite few. When I was a child and someone passed, I remembered you made food and you visited them. You sat around in a house full of people and told stories about your experience with the deceased. When my dad passed, people asked me what I wanted. I said food because I was sure that friends and family would flood the house with visits. I was wrong. We had food at the house and no one to eat it. Initially, I was a little upset, but when I thought about it, I realized several things. First and foremost, this was not the south. Secondly, my father was aged and didn't have a "social circle" if you will. Next, I was at a new place of employment where people didn't really know me that well, and last but certainly not least, the most mind-jolting reality is that I had not been present for many people either. So, there you go; the confession of a griever. I signed cards and generously contributed money. I may have texted or sent a message on social media, but that was the extent of it. I never knew the importance of one's presence during their time of grieving until I experienced it myself. I'm sure I am not the only one who has had this epiphany.

I always went by the rule that if I didn't have your telephone number or know where you lived then it was inappropriate to come to your house at such a sensitive time. I have, since, reconsidered my theory. I appreciated the acts of kindness from people who didn't normally and personally interact with me. It may have been a visit, a card, or a meal sent over through someone else. Whatever the act was, I was humbled and grateful. I still believe that there is some level of validity to my theory, but I also now know there are other ways to be present.

When my mom passed, we had a constant flow of visitors. Again, not the folks I thought would be there. Granted, we were in the middle of the COVID-19 pandemic, so I will attribute the absences of some to that. Honestly, because of the danger involved, I didn't want many visitors. I will tell you what blessed my whole soul; something I knew already, but to witness it and to experience it was astonishing: the folks that surrounded my sister and me during my mom's passing weren't all her family. My dad's family showed up like champions. As a child, our families were so close that I could never really tell the difference between mommy's side and daddy's side. It took me to become a whole grown woman before I realized that my Uncle David was my mom's brother and not my dad's brother. Then we had an aunt named Grace, or Aunt Gracie as I affectionately call her. No one could have ever convinced me that she wasn't my mother's aunt. My mom and Aunt Grace were very close. They talked daily and did everything together. It shocked my world when I realized she was my daddy's aunt. In fact, my dear Aunt Gracie was there by my mother's side every day while she was ill, and she was there to see her take her last breath. I don't know which moment hurt my heart the worst—knowing that my mom had just taken her last breath or seeing the sadness in my Aunt Gracie's eyes when she realized her best friend had just left her. It was such a heart-wrenching moment for me. How do you live on past this kind of hurt? At that moment, I saw that I wasn't the only one who had to figure out the answer to that question. Although the question still remains in my mind, my dear auntie answered that question in her own way. Just a few short weeks after my mother's death, she passed due to complications of COVID-19. To see how she sat by my mother's and countless others' bedsides for years, I was crushed to know that she was in the hospital alone when it was her time to go. How does one deal with such hurt when your heart believed that the God of your salvation would raise her up?

How, when you rehearsed a testimony of victory day after day?

How, when there was no time to prepare for this moment?

How, when the comforting embrace of another human being has been snatched away by the threat of this evil disease called coronavirus?

Just HOW?

There is an answer in the Word of God for this. I just could not hear it.

The Lord is close to the brokenhearted and saves those who are crushed in spirit.

Psalms 34:18

Fear not, for I am with you; be not dismayed, for I am your God; I will strengthen you, I will help you, I will uphold you with my righteous right hand.

Isaiah 41:10

Rule 4: Say what you can do and do what you say

Most won't admit this, but most times when we say we will pray for someone, it is only at that moment that we think of that person and really feel empathy for them. We have good intentions, but as you scroll down your timeline and see someone has experienced a loss, you respond with a message, and you keep scrolling. How many of you can honestly say that you really take the time to pray for their healing? Pray for their process? Pray that they have all they need financially, emotionally, and spiritually to successfully walk through their period of mourning and grief? Think about it. I'm not talking about a general prayer we may utter at night, asking God to bless all the bereaved. I mean really taking some time to be specific and intentional about your prayers. Be honest. If I were to take an honest poll, I truly believe that the favor would weigh heavily on the "no" side of the scale. This is not okay, yet it is okay. It is okay because it is something that, once it is realized, can be easily changed.

I remember the moment God brought this to my attention. I messaged someone and said "praying for you, "as I read their post about the loss of a loved one. I clearly remember hearing God whisper in my ear, "When?" I was confused and ready to remind God how I diligently pray for…oh yea. God had a point. I wasn't praying for them. I was simply acknowledging their loss.

We must learn to transition from intention to action in our prayers for the grievers. Prayer is not just saying to God "bless this person and heal their hurt." Prayer is still a conversation, right? So, perhaps, we should approach it in that manner. Yes, it is okay to make your request known, but to complete a prayer, you must also allow God to speak to you. It's called dialogue. Perhaps He will show you how to be of value

47

to a griever. Perhaps He will tell you to take a basketball court and put it in their yard to give the kids an outlet.

As a believing griever, we are counting on your prayers. I could literally feel the prayers of some of my friends. There were pastors whose voices I heard in my sleep, praying for me. True prayers reach our hearts. They lift us, and they give us strength. Please, do what you say and really pray.

People mean well. God knows we do. If you are not one of great chariness, I would like to encourage you to please watch what you promise a griever. This is not the time to be a promise-breaker. It is not a time to be emotionally driven. Limit your verbal commitments. Don't tell someone to call you if they need help and then, when they call, you are too busy to stop and help. Don't say "I am praying for you," but then never really pray. I find that this is the most common letdown during a time like this. Folks will flood your social media timeline with prayer hands, messages that say, "I'm praying for you," and they never really pray. Ask me how I know. I have been guilty as charged.

During my initial grieving period, I was in a haze. While I do remember some of the heartfelt condolences, most of it went to the wind. The ones I absolutely remember are those who reached out after the fact. There were a few who recognized, after it was all said and done and when all the fanfare had passed, that what I needed the most was support. The check-in calls and the "thinking of you" texts were nourishing to my healing. I am not saying don't be there when the loss first happens—grievers need to feel supported—but please don't forget to circle back a week later, a month later, a year later. It still hurts. Many of us still have to contend with the business of our loved ones. Many have to clear out their belongings. There is so much involved. Be sensitive; offer to help but don't be forceful. Simply let them know you are there, then actually be there. Buy a box of contractor bags or some bins. Offer to pay for a truck rental to move things, buy a memento box for them to keep special memories or photos. Be present.

Sentiments of a Grieving Heart

Below you will find random sentiments extracted from social media or personal conversations I have had with people who have lost loved ones during this pandemic. I place these here so that you know that you are not alone. I have even included a few of the sentiments of consolation that I thought were very appropriate.

- Still heartbroken. God, I am wounded and need your healing. God continues to heal me through prayer and fasting. Thank you in advance.

- My soul is still weakened every day thinking about my Dad #stillbroken #heartbreak #crushed Most people will never know I'm shattered for real. I honestly don't know how I'm still functioning, but when you see me, you will see the smile and the laugh.

- Sundays will never be the same (heartbroken).

- I know I have been invited to a lot of places so far. I do apologize for not showing up. I lost my father this year—my rock and my everything. Life has not been the same.

- All these deaths! So sad. So sad.

- Some people just can't handle your pain. That's why I try to mask it.

49

- As tears begin to fall, this being the first Father's Day without you here, I'm so grateful to have had such an amazing father in my life. This morning I had an epiphany: all the times you gave me tough love and I felt like you were being unfair to me over my siblings, I realized that you expected more of me because I am your first born and you were training me up for times like this; to be strong but also relevant in the world. Daddy, I get it now...lol. Happy Heavenly Father's Day

- Man, this is about to be another night crying myself to sleep. This will never be okay.

- God, forgive me because my hurt is turning into anger.

- As I reflect over 2020, I think of my loved ones that have passed away and so much pain it has caused due to illness, COVID-19, and being murdered. But I truly know that God has it all in His hands. I thank God for allowing me to cherish memories that I will always hold onto in my heart.

- This griever got a reminder on their Google reminder to send their mom some love on her birthday. This hits differently when you can no longer call, visit, or celebrate your parents. Happy heavenly birthday, mom. Cherish your parents while they're here.

- I want everybody around and no one around all at the same time.

- I cried so hard when everyone left. I kept telling them that I was okay.

- It was a continuous hit of people who lost their mom. Are all moms dying? Am I going to die too?

50

- Always beautiful, on both the inside and the outside. When your new norm is life without your mommy but she was a major part of my entire life... Not a day went by that I didn't talk to my girl, several times a day. #brokenhearted #lifeillneverbethesame #myworld #wehadsomanyplans #thatsmile #ilostmybestfriend #hugyourmom

- I am devastated to see this. I feel like I am stuck in a bad dream. I'm so sorry to hear that you lost both your mother and sister in one week. Sending you all my love and prayers right now.

- You and your family did an amazing job taking care of mom and making sure her days were enjoyable. As you celebrate her life, the joy of the Lord Shall be your strength!

- Sis, I am in deep prayer for you all. I have rewritten this post several times and I know my shock pales in comparison to your family's grief. May God send you comfort and peace over you and your entire family.

- Yesterday was rougher than I expected without you mom. (brokenhearted) I hope you enjoyed the Easter card I got you. I know how much you used to love your cards. Life hasn't seemed real without you especially yesterday and I know it will never be the same. Nonetheless, we know you want us to keep living, being great, and making priceless memories. I'll keep trying my best to push through. Until we are reunited again, keep watching over us. Love you always and forever My Girl/Mommy/My Heart. Real love never dies. (Tears)

51

You might get stuck!

A friend of mine passed away from COVID. I was hurt because I had not spoken with her and had plans to call her the day she passed.

Her mother, a beautiful soul, passed away from cancer on a Wednesday. Her death was somewhat anticipated because she was suffering for quite some time and both my friend and her sister had solicited prayers via social media. I saw the request, and, like most, posted a few words of encouragement on their timeline. When I saw the announcement that her mom had passed, I was saddened, of course. This time, I understood the depth of her pain. Being a student of my own lessons, I didn't call immediately because I wanted to give myself time to really think about how to be a good consoler. I wanted to make an impact, so I wanted time to self-assess and determine what I could reasonably offer and, hopefully, not do or say some of the non-helpful things I experienced.

The following Saturday, I was informed that my friend had also passed away from COVID. I was in utter shock. I was devastated. I was confused. I felt the biggest sense of regret that I had not called and given my condolences. Later, I found out that my friend had contracted COVID along with a few other family members, including her father who was in the hospital battling COVID in a major way. Because she had COVID and because of the pandemic, she was unable to be by her mother's side during her transition. She was home, in quarantine, along with her sister, who also had COVID. This was the worst of the worst scenarios to me. Understand that my friend and her mother passed just three days apart and their beloved husband and father was touch and go.

I spoke with her sister, whom I also consider a friend, and I was stuck. I had no sensible words to share. What could I say to someone who had just lost their mother, their sister, and was unsure about the status of her father? What do you say to someone who is made to quarantine alone and away from their spouse and children because of the coronavirus? She had just lost her two best friends and could not even feel the embrace of the true loves she had left.

No words would exit my mouth when she called me about 6:30 am just because she needed someone to talk to. All I could do was listen as I cried silently on the other end of the line, trying not to upset her further. I wanted to pray with her, but what would I say? I wanted to give conscious and comforting words, but what would they be? All I could do was listen and, sparingly, utter a few careful words just to let her know I was fully engaged in the conversation. When I got off the telephone with her, I felt totally useless. I felt like I had grossly failed that moment.

This experience reminded me that when you think your life is bad, you should take a moment to hear someone else's story. You will always find a place for gratitude. Here I was devastated that my mother and father passed two months shy of a year apart and this person lost two people just three days apart. At least I was able to be there by both my mom and my dad's side when they passed. She couldn't be there. I'm still very sad for her. No one should have to experience such great loss so close together. Not only were the deaths close together but to have to suffer them while in isolation is devastating!

The power of the human touch has been stripped away from many of us during this pandemic. As much as I have studied and written about grief, coping skills, and being a "good consoler," I got stuck. The devastation of the moment overtook me, so I was not an effective consoler to this young lady. A situation may occur when all the right words may not flow. It's okay. Forgive yourself and move forward in your efforts to console.

Good Grief!

Lesson Learned: get to know the people you love in a more meaningful way. I find myself wishing I had asked more questions and made note of more facts. There seem to be so many holes in the story of their life. Listening to the inside stories of friends and family is both heartwarming and actually kind of heartbreaking at the same time. Why had I not heard these stories before? It makes me feel as if I didn't really know them.

Helping Children Address Grief

Oh, the children! If we don't learn anything else in this process, learn not to forget the children. So many times, during our own grief, we forget that our children are suffering just as much, if not more than we are. They have also suffered a loss. If the person was dear to you, more than likely, the child loved them as well. The difference is that you have the mental capacity to understand death. Most children do not. Not only must they walk through the loss, but their rock, you, are not present. Though they are resilient creatures, they need ways to sort grief as well. It does not just roll off of them the way we would like to think it does.

I remember when my grandmother died. I felt very left out. I was a young adult but those who were planning her funeral were all older and did not consider me.

When my dad and mom passed, I asked my 12-year-old son how he felt. I encouraged him and my grandchildren to be a part of the memorial service. Unfortunately, due to COVID, they could not attend my mother's service, but they were allowed to contribute ideas to her birthday celebration, which was a week later. We took their ideas and made them happen so that they felt a part of the process.

I asked my son, months later, after my mom passed, how he felt, and his answer was much different. At the time of my mother's death, he didn't say much of anything. He kept saying he was fine, or he shrugged his shoulders as if to say he didn't know how he felt. Later, he said he didn't believe it and that he was sad.

My daughter reacted as I thought she would. She took it pretty hard, but we were all glad she found someone to travel over 800 miles with her and that she made it to see my mom before she passed. In fact, I believe my mom waited for her and the kids to get there. She passed about four hours after my daughter got there.

A delayed reaction of my daughter was regret. My mom had been asking her to move to the small town where she lived, and my daughter kept saying she would consider it but never did.

Many times, when loved ones pass away, this thing called regret taunts us. We think "what if I could have done more" or "I should have said this." It's very common, especially with those who live a distance from their loved ones and did not get to see them often. Take some time to consider the children (young or older) in your circle. They will need a guide as they manage their grief. Often, they have had very little or no major losses and are not equipped to process their feelings without assistance. Regret for them can easily spill over and become lifelong anxiety.

I have many of my own regrets, most of which are wanting to have had more meaningful conversations. I also regret that I did not get to "repay" my mother, especially for all the sacrifices she made.

I wanted to pay her house off and take her on vacations or send her allowances each month to live carefreely. Unfortunately, none of these things happened. In my mind, she left me too soon, but regret spoke to me and said "no, you moved too late." Moving beyond that regret has been an ongoing labor of healing and acceptance.

The Aftermath of Death

Once all the fanfare is over, the last song has been sung, and when all of the people have gone away, there it stands: the darkest day. No one is bringing a meal by, yet you still don't have the inspiration to prepare one of your own. No one is calling to see if you need a ride or a sitter, yet you still have business to complete on behalf of your loved one. You still have their closets to empty or their home to clear. There are legal matters, accounts to close, bills to handle, and the list goes on.

Attention consolers: this is when we really need you! We need strength and support as we face the dark days ahead. We may sound strong on social media, and we may be able to fake our way through a brief telephone call, but if you take a few extra moments to really connect and look beyond our learned smile or beyond our dry eyes, you will see the hurt and the agony we behold each day. It is more than the major things, such as dealing with court cases or deciphering through a will. It is things like seeing that piece of mail with their name on it or hearing their voice on a voicemail. It's getting that telephone call or bumping into someone on the street who was not aware of your loved one's passing and having to tell them that they are deceased then being forced into consoling them in their shock and or embarrassment for not knowing.

This is all considered the aftermath. It's unavoidable. Think about ways to support the griever beyond the obvious time of bereavement.

In Conclusion...

At this moment, I still have some very challenging days. There are moments where I am accepting of my parents' death and other times when the foundation of my faith is rattled. I experience bouts of sadness, confusion, and even regret. The regret is because I don't feel that I celebrated my loved ones in the manner they deserved. For instance, my father served in the military, and I never really rolled out the fanfare for him, recognizing him as a veteran while he was alive. I'd also dreamed for many years of paying off my mother's house and allowing her to spend her golden years in leisure and ease, repaying her for the sacrifices she made raising her family. But I never got there. Some days this is all okay. Some days it haunts me.

What helps me when I am feeling down is supporting others in need. I help seniors by buying them food, sending them flowers, and making sure they know someone is thinking about them. I also reach out to others who have experienced loss by doing a check-in at significant times such as birthdays, holidays, or anniversaries. It helps me deal with my own grief better if I am being a consoler to another griever. I can truly say that consoling others heals me.

The other tool I use to aid in my grief is talking about it. I know some people would rather not because it hurts, but, for me, it is helpful to talk about how I am feeling; talking about those moments when my loved one is on my mind or when I have a rough day. Sharing stories or even having mini meltdowns in the presence of those who are close to me helps. I don't want to hide my pain. I believe that I should be able to grieve out loud if I want to. I'm not looking for attention I'm just being very transparent. I believe that my transparency allows those in my life to deal with me on a more real level, and it also helps others who are experiencing the same feelings to be free with how they are coping. I am a firm believer that knowing and seeing others overcome a challenge offers hope to the onlooker.

I have really struggled with how to end this book. Each time I thought I was done, I was visited by more personal loss. I kept having more experiences that I felt needed to be included in this work. However, what I know for sure is that I cannot include enough personal anecdotes to take the sting out of what you may be going through. You will take what you already know, pair it with the wisdom in this book, and develop your own process. If that process is even a tiny bit easier for having spent this time reading this book, then my purpose has been fulfilled.

I really hope that this book has inspired the consoler in you, validated the griever in you, and has been and will continue to be an instrument by which you feel supported in whatever role you find yourself in at this moment. Share this book, document your journey, heal, and be healed by the power of "GOOD GRIEF"!

Poem: GOOD GRIEF

Can grief ever be good?

Can the two words be appropriately paired in a sentence together?

What exactly is so good about my grief?

They say that if I grieve, it indicates that I have loved.

They say that if I am able to love, that it is good.

It is better to have loved and experience grief; or is it better to have never loved and know no grief?

This is what I ponder; this is the answer I seek.

I guess I can agree; the love I have experienced is powerful and my life would not be what it is today had I not experienced it.

Yet, I guess I can also agree that one cannot miss what they never knew, and if I never knew love, I would never feel the pain that has stricken my heart in such a fierce manner.

To love or not to love is what must be settled.

Whoa, it is too late for me to choose not to love, for I am of God and God is love.

I was born of love; therefore, I must grieve.

For my love was and is good; therefore, I will have "GOOD GRIEF".

TRIBUTE TO MY DAD, WILLIAM D. EVANS 1945-2019

S o, the book of William D. Evans is now closed. There are so many lessons embodied in the pages.

I've had the opportunity to revisit a few chapters through reminiscent conversations with those who knew and loved you. Each page is full of life lessons for me to glean. The early chapters begin with a lesson on discipline and independence. It talks about how you left home as a young man, joined the military, got married, and started a family—all away from the life you knew in the south. Chapter two speaks to your entrepreneurial spirit. Your success as a skilled and talented electrician exemplifies courage and confidence. Then there are lessons on character, such as forwardness, loyalty, and friendship. The one I love most is the chapter that highlights your love for family. I enjoy hearing all the stories about how much your family admired you. You tried all you could to live up to the expectations of everyone, and when you could no longer do it, you were crushed.

Each chapter so explicitly outlines your intelligence, your well-roundedness, and your impeccable character. I believe the best thing we can do as your heirs is to try to mirror your chapters on life. I'd like to think that, in some ways, our lives have already begun to reflect your chapters. We don't claim that you or your life was perfect. This is evident through the battles you fought through. But we do proclaim that you were the perfect son, nephew, cousin, and friend to those who loved you.

I guess it is up to us who are left behind to write the sequel. It's entitled, "How to live a life without a dad." The first chapter begins now. I am one of the fortunate ones who did not have to experience life without having their dad around. That is a blessing I will never take for granted. My first chapter.

A world without a dad... Who does this? I can't believe I now have to live in a world without the **only** man who truly loved me. Who is going to take me in their arms and dance with me the way you did? Who is going to protect me? Whose shoulder do I cry on when my heart is broken? Even in my adult years, I remember coming to visit you in the nursing home and lying next to you in your bed with tears flowing down my face. You really couldn't say a word, and I'm not even sure you understood, but you were there and that's all I really needed. Since day one, and for as long as you could be, you were always there. You were there to see me take my first breath, and, consequently, I was blessed to be there to see you take your last.

Dad, your book may be closed, but your story will go on. Your legacy will never be forgotten. Tamara will carry your intelligence and your exceptionally particular ways. Ashlee will carry your passion for life and your loyalty to friends. Jordan will carry your mild-mannered spirit with a natural instinct to protect those he loves. A'myree will carry your forwardness and your unwavering confidence in her own knowledge, and Egypt the warrior in you. She is as sweet as pie but will cut you if she has to. As for me, I vow to carry your heart for service to mankind.

Well, Poppie! Rest on. We have big shoes to fill, but we will do our best to not only carry your legacy but also expand it. I love you, dad.

CELEBRATION OF LIFE FOR

William D. Evans

Sunrise
June 3, 1945

Sunset
May 8, 2019

- MEMORIAL SERVICE -
Saturday, May 18, 2019
Service 11:30 a.m.

Yarborough and Rocke Funeral Home
1001 North 63rd Street - Philadelphia, PA 19151
Elder Tyrone Curtis, Eulogist

TRIBUTE TO MY MOM, CLARA M. EVANS 1947-2020

Mom, I still cannot believe you are gone. You slipped away so quickly. My heart has realized it, but my mind will not accept it. I have so many questions to ask. I was working so hard to be able to upgrade your retirement. I wanted your latter days to be filled with joy and laughter. I often wonder if you ever really experienced joy in its fullest capacity. As I reflect on your life, all I see is hard work and sacrifice. You gave your life to please others, but mom, were you happy? I knew I couldn't have you forever, but I just wanted you to be here long enough to reap all that you sowed. I wanted to hear that childlike laughter, to see that beautiful smile, and to hear your heartbeat like thunder because of your inner joy. Mom, I'm sorry. I'm sorry that I moved too slow to reach a point where I could give you what you deserved. Mom, I'm sorry I was so consumed with my own life that I couldn't be the reason you smiled each day. I was so busy trying to keep my own head above the water that I didn't see you drowning. Mom, I'm sorry. I truly hope that what they say is true; I hope you have some sense of consciousness to be able to see me now. I am going to make you proud. The imprint you have left on my heart will be left in this world. You were quiet but you were powerful. You were loving, you were compassionate, and you were full of faith. The world will know you through me. I will transcend all of who you were through the work I do during whatever time I have left. Watch me if you can. I love you, mom.

Home Going Celebration
for the Late

Clara Evans

Sunrise: May 4, 1947 — Sunset: April 27, 2020

Wednesday May 6, 2020
11:00 A.M.
National Cemetery
803 E. Cemetery Road
Florence, SC 29506

LEGACY LEFT. LEGACY RECEIVED. LEGACY MOVING FORWARD.

God Bless

Someone dear to you has gone away; there are no soothing words anyone can say

This little note is just to say. It's okay, NOT to be okay.

Upon the initial news, the calls came in, the prayers went up and your FB and IG were blown up. You may have even experienced some brief moments of normalcy.

"She" was there by your side as you knew she would be, dotting every "I" and crossing every "T" But even her comfort can't reach that place within thee.

You try to convince yourself to go on because as we all say he is in a better place.

So each day you somehow manage to rise up and put on your face

The real is... you are still in shock and still very much in pain;

people don't understand that your life has forever changed.

You look around and everyone's life is still the same. They are going on with their daily task and in silence, you operate painfully under the mask. People expect you to be strong and it's wrong.

Honestly, I can't say I know your pain because I don't. I do feel your pain and it's deep.

I know my time to experience it is closer than I want to admit. I just hope that there is someone around to tell me that it's okay to NOT be okay.

I just wanted to say to you sis, cry when you want to, scream when you want to, be angry if you need to be...do whatever will help you through a healthy grieving process. Take as long as you need and feel free NOT to be okay.

Love you. I'm here if you ever need to just "Not Be Okay"

THANK YOU!

Tamara Evans, my sister, for your support and confidence in my ability to write this book.

Ashlee Morgan, my daughter, for her inspiration and her diligence in helping to promote this writing. Your confidence in me means the world.

Bishop Steven Walker, my pastor, for his continued prayers, his wisdom and encouragement. When I was stuck and or discouraged, your wisdom helped me push through and "get it did!"

Pastors Whitney and Terri Blunden and the A Place Called Restoration Church family for their prayers and outreach during the passing of my loved ones. I literally heard your voices calling my name.

Apostle Sharon Wright for her words of encouragement and daily prayers during the passing of my mother. You literally snatched me out of the grip of depression.

All the participants of my roundtable discussion who allowed me to share their stories with the world. Your participation pushed this work to a new level of excellence.

Frederick Fields, my videographer and editor. Your sacrifices are immeasurable. Your friendship is invaluable.

My publisher and editors at Bird House Publishing for guiding, respecting, and perfecting my work throughout this process.

This book would not be the treasure it is without each one of you. Thank you.

JOURNEY JOURNAL

Sometimes it's good to document our process. Here are a few prompts to help you along your journey. You can use these prompts or use some of your own. Feel free to use a separate sheet of paper to write your thoughts. Never let the special moments you had fade away. Keep them alive by documenting your journey towards healing.

When _____ passed away, I immediately felt…

_____

_____

_____

_____

I miss them most when…

_____

_____

_____

_____

The thing that comforts me the most is…

_____

_____

_____

Whenever I feel overcome with grief I will…

_____

_____

_____

The most difficult time for me is…

_____

_____

_____

I can honor their legacy by…

_____

_____

_____

_____

The most memorable moment I have is…

_____

_____

_____

_____

If I had to describe my loved one in one sentence, it would be…

_____

_____

_____

If I had one more day with my loved one I would…

_____

_____

_____

_____

I feel most connected to my loved one when…

_____

_____

_____

_____

A song that makes me think of my loved one is _____
_____ because…

_____

_____

_____

_____

Something that would have made me feel better when my loved one
died was…

_____

_____

_____

_____

Do you have any unanswered questions about your loved one? If yes,
list them.

_____

_____

_____

_____

What emotion do you feel most in your grief?

_____

_____

_____

What has been most helpful to you in your grieving process?

_____

_____

_____

Don't let your journaling end with these prompts. Move beyond this. Write your loved one a letter. Paint a picture that represents how you felt with them in your life, then do another one depicting how you feel without them. Write a poem. Create an event that honors who they are or what they represented.

ABOUT THE AUTHOR

P amela Evans was educated in the Philadelphia public school system. Upon completion of high school, she graduated from Dorthea B. Lane Business School, then went on to the Community College of Philadelphia where she studied English and Theater. She eventually attended the University of Phoenix where she studied Business Administration. Pamela then went on to further her education and attended Lincoln University and graduated with her master's degree in Human Services.

Pamela loves people and getting to know them beyond what meets the eye. She enjoys engaging in conversations that allow others to address deep-rooted issues which prevent them from being their best selves. She aims to love those in her life unconditionally with hopes that it will help them through any hurt they may encounter. Pamela has a strong passion for service to both children and seniors and loves to serve her community by advocating for a better quality of life. She also loves writing life-impacting poetry that seeps deeper than a simple rhyme.

Pamela believes that living her life transparently and being her authentic self is the best way to maintain her happiness. While she found parenting to be a great challenge in today's society, she loves both her children dearly and aims to create an open and loving relationship with her two children. While she states that her children are her heartbeats, she also proclaims that being a grandmother is a whole new level of love. She absolutely adores being a "Nuna" as her two grandchildren affectionately call her.

In writing this book, Pamela hopes to help readers identify where they are in the grieving process, validate their process, become more sensitive towards those who are grieving, build deep and meaningful relationships with loved ones, and become more purposeful consolers. She hopes that with the completion of this work, readers will begin a healthy journey towards healing and finding the good in their grief.

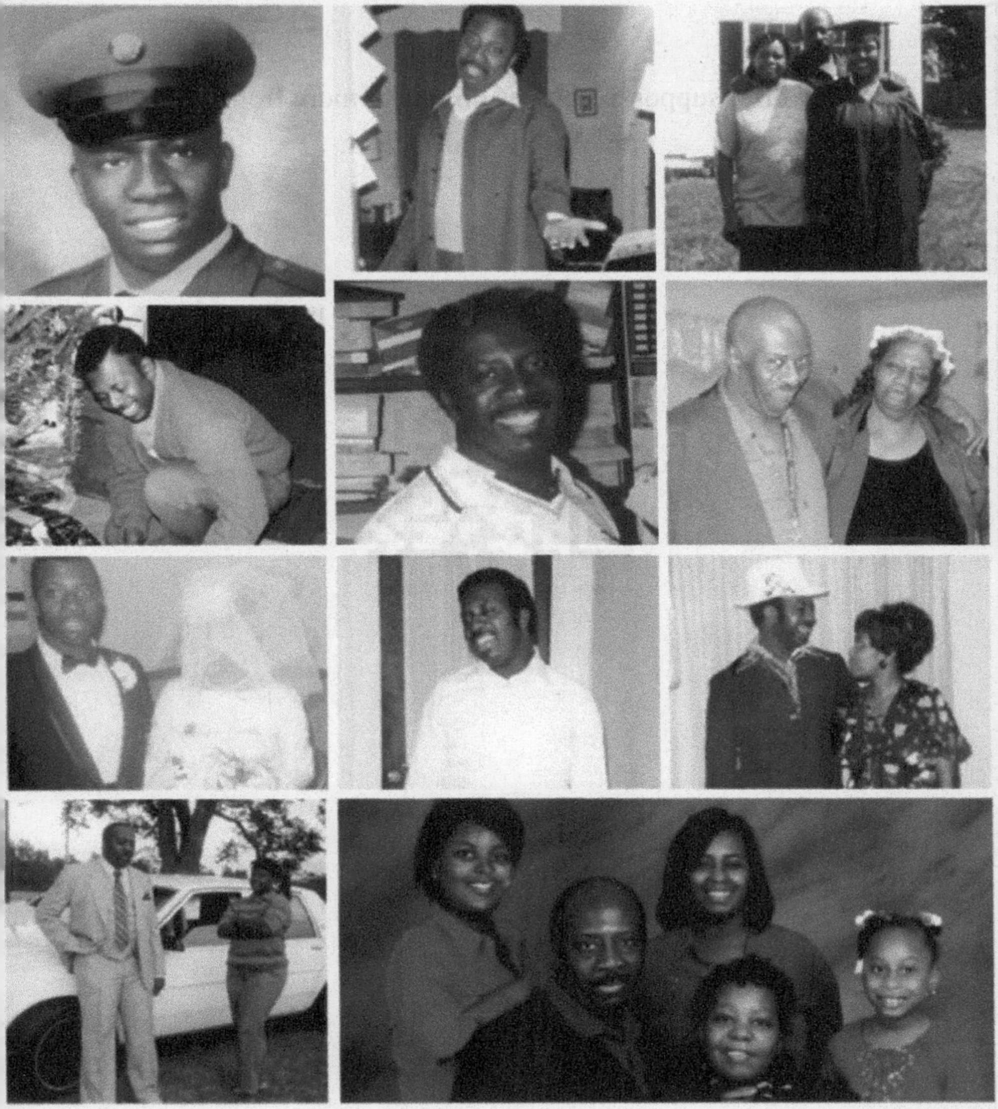

For more grief support resources or to hear more from this author scan the QR code below.

www.pamelatevans.com

CPSIA information can be obtained
at www.ICGtesting.com
Printed in the USA
LVHW041307130222
711036LV00015B/925

9 781734 321777